VANESSA WILLIAMS'S QUEEN OF TIMELESS BEAUTY:

Age-Defying Wisdom and Beauty Secrets

Linda A. Walker

TABLE OF CONTENT

8:2 Personal Stories of Transformation and Empowerment

CONCLUSION

INTRODUCTION

This is "Vanessa Williams's Queen of Timeless Beauty: Age-Defying Wisdom and Beauty Secrets." We explore the legendary Vanessa Williams' unmatched grace and timeless appeal in this engrossing voyage. As the self-proclaimed "Queen of Timeless Beauty," Vanessa shares her age-defying knowledge and reveals the trade secrets that have kept her glamorous glow intact throughout the years.

Come along with us as we investigate the essence of ageless beauty, breaking through social conventions and accepting the wisdom that comes with aging. Vanessa's journey turns into a lighthouse that helps us tap into our inner strength and cultivate inner brightness as the cornerstone of timeless beauty.

You'll go on a life-changing journey via the pages of this book, discovering Vanessa's skincare practices, makeup tricks, exercise regimens, and style staples that have characterized her renowned elegance. Experience the beauty that transcends national boundaries as we delve into global influences and reinterpret beauty norms. Let go of limitations and embrace the path to self-love and self-assurance.

This is more than simply a beauty manual; it's an encouragement to rewrite your own story of beauty, a celebration of uniqueness, and a tribute to the power that comes from accepting change. Vanessa Williams's timeless beauty philosophy becomes your road map to age-defying radiance with her exclusive interviews, personal tales, and abundance of useful advice.

Prepare to travel to a place where beauty has no bounds and transcends time. The timeless beauty queen is ready to impart her knowledge to you and encourage a life filled with grace, self-assurance, and endless charm. Your journey to timeless beauty starts right now.

CHAPTER 1: WHO IS Vanessa Williams

Vanessa Williams is a well-known and diverse individual with a broad impact on advocacy, beauty, and entertainment. Tarrytown, New York was the place of Vanessa Lynn Williams' birth on March 18, 1963. She broke down barriers and made a lasting impression on the world.

In 1983, she became well-known after becoming the first African-American woman to win the Miss America title, which was a significant turning point in the pageant's history. Vanessa's successful career was paved with her tenacity and grace in the face of adversity during her reign.

Vanessa is a talented artist in many different mediums. She is a Grammy-nominated recording artist who has demonstrated her vocal versatility by creating albums and singles that have reached the top of the charts. Songs

like "Colors of the Wind" and "Save the Best for Last"
have made her a household name in the music business.

Vanessa Williams is a well-known actor who has acted in
movies and television. Her roles in hit TV shows
including "Ugly Betty," "Desperate Housewives," and
"Soul Food" have made her well-known. Among the
well-known movies she has worked on are "Eraser" and
"Shaft."

In addition to her successes in entertainment, Vanessa is
well-known for her advocacy activities. Her prominence
in the beauty and health industry can be attributed to her
dedication to age-inclusive beauty, empowerment, and
shattering social standards.

Vanessa Williams is a trailblazer as well as a
representation of talent, tenacity, and classic beauty. Her
transition from the Miss America stage to a diverse artist
and advocate personifies the idea of shattering
stereotypes and reinventing expectations.

1:1 Early life and background

On March 18, 1963, Vanessa Lynn Williams was born in Tarrytown, New York, in the United States. Her early years were spent in a nurturing and creative setting. Vanessa's parents, Milton and Helen Williams, supported her artistic endeavors after seeing her early aptitude.

Vanessa developed her acting, dancing, and singing abilities at the High School of Performing Arts in New York City during her adolescence. Her eventual success in the entertainment sector was made possible by her early exposure to the performing arts.

It was during her undergraduate years when Vanessa's interest in beauty pageants became apparent. She majored in musical theater while attending Syracuse University. She made history in 1983 when she was crowned Miss America, the first African-American woman to do so. This ground-breaking accomplishment was a turning point in her life and the Miss America pageant's history.

Even though Vanessa's victory was historic, she had to deal with criticism and difficulties while she was Miss America. Vanessa resigned from the position due to controversial situations, but her perseverance and fortitude demonstrated that her career could not be defined by failures.

Her upbringing and early years not only demonstrated her creative abilities but also set the stage for Vanessa Williams to become a leader in the entertainment sector. Vanessa's journey, from her early involvement in the performing arts to her ground-breaking accomplishments, demonstrates a blend of skill, tenacity, and a spirit of innovation that would define her future undertakings.

1:2 The Foundation Of Timeless Beauty

The foundation of the Vanessa Williams Foundation of Timeless Beauty is the idea that genuine beauty comes from the inside out. This foundation's core thesis is that the base of timeless appeal is the importance of cultivating inner brightness. As the driving force behind this idea, Vanessa Williams offers her profound thoughts on confidently and gracefully embracing each stage of life.

This foundation acknowledges that beauty is a comprehensive idea that includes mental health, accepting oneself, and having a positive attitude toward aging rather than being limited to outward appearances. Vanessa's journey turns into a monument to the transformational power that results from cultivating a solid foundation based on self-love and appreciating the beauty present in each new chapter of life.

Vanessa recognizes the individuality that every person brings to the world and encourages people to go on a personal journey of self-discovery through the Foundation of Timeless Beauty. Vanessa is dedicated to enabling others to feel confident and beautiful at every age, which is why she places a strong emphasis on mindfulness, self-care, and leading a balanced lifestyle.

The Foundation of Timeless Beautiful aims to carry on Vanessa Williams's legacy by encouraging people all around the world to rethink what constitutes beautiful, reject age-based prejudices, and embrace the richness that accompanies aging. It is a light of wisdom that leads people to recognize their uniqueness and the timeless beauty that is within each of us.

Essentially, the Vanessa Williams Foundation of Timeless Beauty empowers people to age with grace, confidence, and an unwavering sense of self-worth by offering a holistic approach to beauty that goes beyond cultural expectations. It is not only a celebration of outward elegance.

1:3 Inner Radiance: Nurturing Beauty from Within

 Nurturing Beauty from Within". It reflects the deep realization that genuine beauty originates from a position of confidence, self-love, and optimism. This idea emphasizes how developing inner brightness lays the groundwork for timeless beauty.

Vanessa believes that true beauty is nurtured from within, and it extends beyond cosmetics and skincare regimens. It explores the core of the individual, highlighting the importance of mental and emotional health in the search for classic beauty. This idea encourages people to value their individuality and acknowledges that genuine appeal is largely derived from genuineness.

To achieve inner radiance, one must practice mindfulness, self-reflection, and a dedication to personal development. Vanessa Williams encourages people to recognize and embrace their abilities, realizing that every stage of life has its distinct beauty. Transcending the surface level of brightness can be achieved by cultivating a positive self-image and appreciating the richness of life's events.

Vanessa encourages people to adopt a comprehensive perspective on beauty through "Inner Radiance," one that is based on resilience and self-acceptance. It's a call to embrace aging as a journey to be cherished rather than feared, give self-care priority, and cultivate thankfulness. By doing this, people might discover an ageless beauty that transcends the material world and radiates inner light.

To put it simply, "Inner Radiance" is a philosophy that promotes perspective-changing and serves as a constant reminder that true beauty arises from loving and appreciating the beauty that exists in every instant of life.

1:4 Mindful Aging: Vanessa's Perspective on Embracing Every Stage

Vanessa's Perspective on Embracing Every Stage" captures Vanessa Williams's insightful perspective on approaching old age with dignity and knowledge. This idea encourages people to embrace aging with mindfulness and positivity, seeing every stage of life as a chance for spiritual and personal development.

Vanessa's viewpoint goes beyond cultural constraints and questions accepted ideas of youth-related beauty. Rather, "Mindful Ageing" honors the distinct beauty that changes with time. It's a call to accept the experiences inscribed on one's canvas of existence, the wrinkles as indicators of a life well lived, and the silver strands as strands of wisdom.

Vanessa uses this idea to push for a different understanding of aging—one that views it as a change rather than a decline. It's an admission that each chapter offers a unique set of delights, lessons, and a more profound comprehension of oneself. The knowledge that accumulates over time becomes a crucial component of one's attraction, adding to a timeless beauty that goes beyond the surface.

"Mindful Ageing" is accepting oneself as one evolves, enjoying the journey, and living in the present. Vanessa Williams encourages people to develop resilience, acceptance, and thankfulness for the chances that come with every phase of life. It's an empowering viewpoint that inspires people to rewrite their stories, rethinking social norms, and appreciate the beauty of who they truly are.

"Mindful Aging" essentially captures Vanessa's revolutionary perspective, in which growing older is not a barrier but rather a blank canvas that may be used to create a masterpiece. It's a tribute to the beauty that grows more profound with time, encouraging people to greet each day with awareness and a spirit that gently accepts every phase of this amazing adventure we call life.

CHAPTER 2: SKINCARE RITUALS FOR AGELESS GLOW

"Vanessa's Skincare Rituals for Ageless Glow" reveals the painstakingly designed beauty routine of the enduring icon, Vanessa Williams. Her beauty philosophy is divided into this area, which contains a wealth of information about how to keep skin looking young and vibrant while defying aging.

Vanessa emphasizes a holistic approach that integrates science, nature, and self-care in her skincare regimens, which go beyond superficial measures. She offers the keys to taking care of skin at every stage, from waking up in the morning to rejuvenating it at night. The focus is on creating a lifestyle that promotes skin health from the inside out as well as on external goods.

Find out about Vanessa's go-to skincare products, customized regimens, and the secrets to her dewy skin. Every component of her skincare routine, from the significance of hydration to the transforming potential of specialized treatments, is intended to accentuate inherent beauty and encourage enduring vitality.

This section guides those looking to create a skincare regimen that fits their particular needs and way of life. Understanding the demands of the skin at different stages and modifying one's routine accordingly is more important than just using products.

Taking care of one's skin is a way to show oneself love, and "Vanessa's Skincare Rituals for Ageless Glow" is an invitation to start a path of self-care. It showcases Vanessa's dedication to encouraging people to see their beauty at any age, showing that skin can have a classic radiance that lasts a lifetime with the correct maintenance.

2:1 Morning and Night Routines: Vanessa's Daily Skincare Regimen

Vanessa's Daily Skincare Regimen" reveals the painstaking and tried-and-true methods that give Vanessa Williams's face an enduring glow. This section functions as a thorough guide and provides an insight into the beauty icon's daily routines meant to nourish and preserve her glowing skin.

Daily Routines:

1. Easy Cleansing: Vanessa starts her day with a mild cleanser that keeps the skin's natural equilibrium intact while getting rid of pollutants that have accumulated overnight.

2. Hydration Boost: The main attraction is a moisturizing serum that makes the skin supple and ready for the day.

3. Sunscreen Protection: Vanessa stresses the value of protecting your skin from UV rays by using a broad-spectrum SPF.

Bedtime Routines:
1. Makeup Removal: To ensure clean skin before bed, the nightly routine begins with a thorough makeup removal procedure.

2. Deep Cleaning: To get rid of the day's impurities and encourage skin renewal, Vanessa uses a deep cleaning procedure.

3. Targeted Treatments: Serums that address particular issues like fine wrinkles or uneven tone are administered at night.

4. Rich Moisturization: To finish the routine, use a nutritious night cream or moisturizer, which gives the skin the nutrition it needs to heal itself overnight.

Vanessa stresses the value of consistency and modifying skincare regimens to meet the changing demands of the skin across both routines. Her dedication to a customized, well-balanced regimen demonstrates a comprehensive view of beauty that emphasizes long-term skin health and self-care.

"Morning and Night Routines: Vanessa's Daily Skincare Regimen" is more than just a list of instructions; it's a guide for anyone trying to create a skincare regimen that fits their schedule and leaves their skin glowing with youth.

2:2 Secrets to Flawless Skin: Tips and Tricks from the Queen of Timeless Beauty

Uncovering the closely kept secrets of Vanessa Williams, the personification of timeless beauty, "Secrets to Flawless Skin: Tips and Tricks from the Queen of Timeless Beauty" This section is a veritable gold mine of knowledge, providing an inside look at the routines that give Vanessa's beautiful skin and ageless glow.

1. Hydration Is Essential: Vanessa stresses how crucial staying hydrated is. Either by drinking lots of water or using hydrating skincare products, keeping skin hydrated is essential to looking beautiful.

2. Regular Cleaning: A fundamental component of Vanessa's regimen is her dedication to frequent, mild cleaning. Eliminating pollutants permits the skin to breathe and makes it easier for nourishing products to be absorbed.

3. Personalized Skin Care: It's important to know one's skin type and requirements. Vanessa promotes a customized strategy, modifying skincare regimens to target particular issues and adjust to the skin's changing needs.

4. Always Wear Sunscreen: Protecting the skin from the sun's damaging rays is a must. Vanessa emphasizes the need to use broad-spectrum SPF every day to prevent premature aging and preserve skin health.

5. Diet High in Nutrients: Vanessa has skin that is immaculate even without topical treatments. She recognizes the significant influence of nutrition on skin health and embraces a diet high in antioxidants, vitamins, and omega-3 fatty acids.

6. Conscious Lifestyle Decisions: Getting enough sleep and managing stress is essential for maintaining good skin. Incorporating relaxation techniques and making sure you get enough sleep are two of Vanessa's suggestions for enhancing general well-being.

7. Intended Interventions: Vanessa is an advocate of using specific treatments, such as masks and serums, to address particular issues, including uneven texture or fine wrinkles. These procedures improve skin radiance by applying an additional layer of care.

8. Internal Cleaning: Vanessa supports the idea of cleansing the skin from the inside out. This entails leading a healthy lifestyle, reducing pollution exposure, and taking into account internal variables that affect skin clarity.

"Secrets to Flawless Skin" is a comprehensive manual for maintaining skin health rather than just a compilation of cosmetic advice. Vanessa Williams's method emphasizes the link between the desire for long-lasting beauty, attentive skincare routines, and internal well-being.

CHAPTER 3: MAKEUP MAGIC: ENHANCING YOUR NATURAL BEAUTY

"Makeup Magic: Enhancing Your Natural Beauty" is an engrossing exploration of Vanessa Williams's revolutionary cosmetics technique, an art form that honors and accentuates each person's inherent beauty. Vanessa offers her knowledge in this part, revealing the techniques behind her hallmark looks and encouraging readers to use cosmetics as a means of self-expression.

1. Honoring Uniqueness: Vanessa's attitude starts with the understanding that each face has its narrative to tell. She views makeup as a tool to bring attention to and enhance certain qualities rather than to cover them up. It's a call to acknowledge and appreciate one's unique beauty.

2. Perfect Basis: Vanessa stresses the significance of using a foundation that complements the skin tone and

blends in effortlessly. The foundation is the canvas on which the rest of the makeup magic is applied.

3. Glistening Eyes: Vanessa's skill in makeup artistry frequently centers on her eyes. To create a captivating glance, she offers advice on highlighting eye shapes, selecting the perfect eyeshadow tint, and perfecting the art of eyeliner.

4. Alluring Lips: Vanessa's approach to lip makeup is about accentuating the natural form and adding a hint of allure, whether she goes for a strong lip color or a delicate nude. She suggests experimenting with different hues to see which suits a person's personality the best.

5. Dynamic Contouring: Vanessa uses contouring techniques to define and shape her face's features while keeping it radiant and natural. Subtle improvements that accentuate the facial contours are more important than drastic makeovers.

6. The Blush Power: Vanessa describes blush as a lovely touch that infuses the complexion with life and vibrancy. She offers advice on how to apply blush correctly and choose the appropriate tone to give one a glowing, healthy complexion.

7. Flexibility and Imagination: Vanessa views makeup as a tool for artistic expression. She exhorts readers to have fun, try out different looks, and modify their makeup for different events, feelings, and personal preferences.

"Makeup Magic" is a tribute to the ability of makeup to change people when applied creatively and with intention. Readers are encouraged to delve into the fascinating world of makeup with the help of Vanessa Williams, learning how it can be a self-confidence booster and a celebration of the innate beauty that makes each person distinctly alluring.

3:1 Vanessa's Signature Makeup Looks

"Vanessa's Signature Makeup Looks" captures the refinement and allure that characterize Vanessa Williams's legendary beauty. Vanessa has a great sense of classic elegance, and she has put together a selection of signature beauty looks that draw attention to her best features and inspire others to embrace their sense of style.

1. Traditional Elegance: Vanessa pays homage to Old Hollywood refinement with her timeless beauty appeal. Imagine bright red lips, flawlessly lined eyes, and well-groomed eyebrows. This classic group perfectly captures the spirit of Hollywood's golden age, radiating confidence and grace.

2. Luminance of Nature: Vanessa embraces her inherent attractiveness and frequently goes for a beautiful, young appearance. A natural lip, a hint of blush to accentuate the cheekbones, and soft, earthy tones on the eyes all

work together to create a look that is easily lovely but subtle.

3. Drama with Smoky Eyes: Vanessa looks quite seductive with her smokey eye makeup. A neutral lip, well-defined lashes, and deep, blended eyeshadows create a powerful, alluring gaze that radiates confidence and mystery.

4. The goddess bronzed: Vanessa's bronze goddess look, with its sun-kissed glow, incorporates warm tones that draw attention to her features. A complexion with golden eyeshadows, contouring bronzer, and a glossy natural lip seems radiant and sun-kissed.

5. Vibrant and Fun Colours: Vanessa's vivid and lively color selections reflect her zest for adventure. Her enthusiasm to accept a varied range of styles is highlighted by her bold eyeshadows, bold lips in rich hues, and daring color combinations, all of which emphasize her lively personality.

6. Genuine and Gentle: Vanessa's delicate makeup, which evokes ethereal beauty, combines pastel colors, delicate shimmers, and a hint of highlighter. Her inherent grace is accentuated by the dreamy, romantic style of her look.

Vanessa's distinctive makeup styles are evidence of her variety and proficiency in the art of beauty. She exudes confidence and strength from the inside out with every appearance. Vanessa Williams encourages people to discover the transforming potential of cosmetics and to express their uniqueness with beauty and grace by sharing these signature looks.

3:2 Choosing the Right Products for Timeless Glam

Vanessa Williams's beauty philosophy revolves around the idea of "Choosing the Right Products for Timeless Glam," which highlights the importance of picking skincare and makeup products that are long-lasting and contribute to timeless elegance. Vanessa offers her advice on how to make decisions in this part that support the quest for timeless beauty.

1. Prioritise Quality Above Quantity Vanessa is an advocate of using judgment while choosing cosmetics, emphasizing quality rather than quantity. Purchasing goods with premium ingredients guarantees that they will not only provide noticeable effects but also enhance the general health and vigor of the skin.

2. Principles of Skincare: A thoughtful skincare regimen is the cornerstone of classic glam. Vanessa emphasizes the value of basic skincare products like cleansers,

serums, and moisturizers that are customized to each person's skin type and intended to provide long-lasting brightness.

3. There is no negotiating sun protection: Vanessa emphasizes the age-old significance of sun protection. Selecting skincare and makeup products with SPF integrated into them protects the skin from UV rays' aging effects, establishing the foundation for long-lasting beauty.

4. Multipurpose Makeup Essentials: Vanessa advocates using makeup that is easy to wear from day to night by choosing classic pieces that are adaptable. Products with several uses, like a neutral eyeshadow palette or a lipstick that goes well on everyone, bring some pragmatism into the glamorous routine.

5. Skin Type Consideration: It's critical to match product selections to an individual's skin type. Vanessa's guidance is focused on products that improve and complement specific skin traits, whether that means

selecting an oil-free formulation for an oily face or a hydrating foundation for dry skin.

6. Classic Colour Scheme: Vanessa's method of doing makeup is choosing a classic color scheme that accentuates the individual's attributes. Timeless colors such as earthy tones, classic reds, and neutral tones provide sophistication and versatility.

7. Mattering Ingredients: Vanessa emphasizes the need to be aware of ingredients. Choosing skin-friendly components over harsh chemicals in skincare products is in line with maintaining long-term skin health and vitality.

8. Adaptation and Trial and error: Being timeless does not equate to stagnant glam. Vanessa promotes flexibility and a spirit of exploration. A dynamic and individualized approach to glamour is ensured by experimenting with new products and modifying the routine to suit changing beauty needs.

In "Choosing the Right Products for Timeless Glam,"
Vanessa Williams shares a mindset that supports the
never-ending pursuit of beauty in addition to helpful
product selection recommendations. Products that
represent the spirit of timeless beauty and not only
improve the skin's overall health but also its external
shine are the focus.

CHAPTER 4: FITNESS AND WELLNESS FOR AGE- DEFYING GRACE

Vanessa Williams Fitness and Wellness for Age-Defying Grace" captures her all-encompassing strategy for preserving style and vigor as she ages. This idea transcends traditional exercise regimens and includes a way of living that nourishes the body and the mind, creating a sense of well-being that adds to an ageless beauty.

Vanessa's approach to fitness places a strong emphasis on the value of continued activity for mental and emotional well-being in addition to physical health. Maintaining a balanced exercise program fosters resilience and a positive attitude in life, serving as a form of self-care. It's about appreciating the beauty in the movement and honoring the body's talents at every stage.

When it comes to ageless elegance, wellness goes beyond physical activity and includes things like diet and awareness. Vanessa Williams promotes a diet that is healthy and well-balanced to enhance general health and beauty. Fitness and well-being work together to create a potent mix that lays the groundwork for long-lasting beauty that results from leading a lively, healthy lifestyle.

"Age-Defying Grace" is a call to embrace health and exercise as enduring allies on the path to self-care. It's about enjoying healthy foods, appreciating physical activity, and adopting habits that support mental and emotional well. Vanessa's concept inspires people to understand the life-changing power of a health-conscious lifestyle as an essential element of timeless elegance.

"Fitness and Wellness for Age-Defying Grace" is essentially a manifestation of Vanessa Williams's dedication to encouraging people to live balanced, active lives that enhance both physical fitness and the glow that results from a strong, resilient spirit. It honors the harmonious relationship between the body and the mind, which lays the groundwork for ageless beauty that transcends all physical constraints.

4:1 Vanessa's Workout Routine: Staying Fit and Fabulous

Vanessa Williams's fitness regimen is evidence of her dedication to maintaining her beauty and fitness at every age. Her program combines cardiovascular, flexibility, and strength training activities to promote overall health and well-being.

1. Strength Training:
-Focusing on Whole-Body Exercises Vanessa incorporates strength- and toning-focused movements that focus on major muscle areas.

  - Bodyweight Exercises: She incorporates efficient bodyweight exercises for muscle endurance and functional strength, such as lunges and squats.

2. Cardiovascular Exercises:

– Dynamic Cardio Workouts: Vanessa works her heart rate up and improves her cardiovascular health by running, cycling, or dancing.

- Interval Training: She incorporates high-intensity interval training (HIIT), which is a quick and efficient method of increasing metabolism and burning calories.

3. Flexibility and Balance:
- Yoga and Pilates: Vanessa uses these practices to maintain her suppleness and enhance her balance. They also help with flexibility.

- Stretching Routine: Consistent stretching sessions help to maintain muscle flexibility, which reduces stiffness and encourages fluid motions.

4. Mindful Practises:
- Mindful Breathing and Meditation: Vanessa practices mindfulness to promote mental clarity and lower stress levels.

- Mind-Body Connection: Mind-body awareness exercises are essential for balancing mental and physical health.

5. Adaptability and Variety:
- Diverse Workouts: Vanessa mixes up her workouts to keep things fresh, ranging from conventional gym sessions to outdoor pursuits.

- Adaptive Approach: Her regimen changes over time to accommodate her body's shifting requirements and maintain sustainability.

Vanessa Williams's approach to exercise emphasizes developing a positive relationship with fitness in addition to the physical components. It represents her conviction that maintaining physical fitness fosters general health, self-assurance, and classic beauty that shines from the inside out in addition to helping one to keep a stunning figure.

4:2 The Role of Nutrition In Timeless Beauty

The Role of Nutrition in Timeless Beauty" confirms Vanessa Williams's theory that the secret to achieving timeless beauty is a well-nourished body. Her perspective on nutrition goes beyond simple nourishment; it's an essential component in the quest for graceful aging and radiant health.

1. Well-Rounded and Full Diet:
 - Focus on Complete Foods: Vanessa places a high value on a diet full of complete, high-nutrient foods such as fruits, vegetables, lean meats, and whole grains.

  - Variety and Colour: For the best possible skin health and vitality, a colorful assortment of fruits and vegetables guarantees a varied variety of vitamins, minerals, and antioxidants.

2. Hydration for Radiance:

- Sufficient Water Consumption: Vanessa bases her beauty regimen on maintaining her hydration, which promotes smooth skin and general well-being.

- Herbal Teas and Infusions: Vanessa uses antioxidant-rich herbal teas to add even more skin-beneficial effects to hydration.

3. Collagen-Boosting Meals:
- Including Collagen-Rich Foods: To promote joint health and skin suppleness, Vanessa includes meals like fish, bone broth, and collagen supplements.

- Vitamins and Minerals: Vital elements that support a youthful complexion include vitamin C, zinc, and copper. These nutrients are also important for the creation of collagen.

4. Intentional Eating Techniques:
- Mindful Eating: Vanessa eats mindfully, appreciating every bite and paying attention to her body's signals of hunger and fullness.

- Emotional Well-Being: Vanessa encourages a positive relationship with food for holistic beauty, understanding the connection between dietary decisions and emotional health.

5. Adaptation to Changing Needs:
- Age-Appropriate Nutrition: Vanessa recognizes that her nutritional needs change as she gets older and modifies her diet to include items that promote vigor and longevity.

- Nutritional Supplements: To ensure a thorough approach to well-rounded health, she may include supplements to address particular nutritional needs.

Vanessa Williams's dietary philosophy is consistent with the notion that beauty is an inward process. The appropriate nutrients may feed the body and help people develop a radiant, age-defying beauty. It's a way of thinking that acknowledges the close relationship between diet, general health, and the ageless beauty that comes from a robust, well-fed body.

CHAPTER 5: STYLE AND ELEGANCE ACROSS TIME

"Style and Elegance Across Time" offers an engrossing examination of Vanessa Williams's legendary fashion career and her ageless method of developing a refined and refined charm. This rule explores Vanessa's style development as well as guides others looking to add timeless elegance to their outfits.

Vanessa's impact on fashion is evidence that style is timeless and not influenced by fads or trends. "Style and Elegance Across Time" honors the skill of dressing with intention, appreciating the value of personal style, and building a wardrobe that captures the essence of each individual. It's an invitation to explore the transforming potential of fashion, where apparel becomes an identity-conveying medium and a vehicle for self-confidence.

This theory examines Vanessa's classic ensembles from across the years, highlighting her ability to transition between different fashion eras with grace and ease. The voyage through "Style and Elegance Across Time" demonstrates the adaptability and versatility that characterize a truly fashionable person, from red carpet splendor to everyday sophistication.

Furthermore, this idea transcends appearances by emphasizing the value of inner confidence in showcasing any style. Vanessa Williams encourages people to enjoy expressing themselves via dress, appreciate their bodies, and try new things with fashion. "Style and Elegance Across Time" is a flexible manual that promotes originality and authenticity in the quest for a fashionable and refined lifestyle rather than a strict set of guidelines.

This idea is essentially a celebration of the timeless appeal that comes from accepting one's stylistic path. It inspires people to view clothing as a vehicle for expressing their unique selves, sharing their tales, and showcasing their innate grace. "Style and Elegance

Across Time" is a tribute to the ability of fashion to change lives, encouraging people to put together a wardrobe that will last and capture the essence of who they are becoming as time goes on.

5:1 Fashion Through the Years: Vanessa's Iconic Looks

"Fashion Through the Years: Vanessa's Iconic Looks" takes readers on a captivating tour of the stylistic development of a real style icon. Vanessa Williams has made a lasting impression on the world of haute couture with her instinct for style. She has demonstrated a dynamic spectrum of looks that exude confidence, refinement, and a timeless sense of beauty.

This investigation starts in the formative years when Vanessa made her debut and won people over with her talent and attractiveness. The trip through each era reveals classic stage looks, red carpet looks, and effortlessly stylish moments that have cemented Vanessa's reputation as a trailblazer in the fashion industry. Every outfit, from the 1980s to the present, conveys a tale about changing fashion trends, individual development, and a dedication to embracing a variety of styles.

Vanessa celebrates originality, confidence, and self-expression through her fashion choices, which go beyond simple attire. "Fashion Through the Years" explores the creativity that goes into every ensemble, from the carefully selected color schemes to the carefully chosen accessories. It explores how Vanessa has used fashion as a medium to convey her complex identity.

This retrospective also shows Vanessa's ability to move across several fashion eras with ease, from the bright and colorful '90s designs to the sleek and contemporary 21st-century looks. She has had a lasting impact on the fashion industry, as seen by her ability to change with the times and still look elegant.

As we go through "Fashion Through the Years," it becomes evident that Vanessa Williams's famous ensembles are ageless displays of grace and sophistication, not limited to any one particular period. This exploration reminds us that fashion is a powerful instrument for fostering confidence and allure across the

changing chapters of life and acts as a sort of
self-discovery, inspiring people to embrace their style
journeys.

5:2 Timeless Wardrobe Essentials for Every Woman

"Timeless Wardrobe Essentials for Every Woman" is a style guide that offers a carefully chosen selection of wardrobe staples that are timeless and transcend trends. It was inspired by Vanessa Williams's timeless sense of style. This way of thinking honors the notion that a well-planned wardrobe reflects a woman's confidence, uniqueness, and ageless elegance in addition to being a statement of fashion.

1. The Traditional White Shirt:

A white shirt that is well-fitting and clean looks great at both informal and formal events. It may be worn with anything from jeans to a fitted suit and acts as a classic blank canvas for a variety of outfits.

2. The Dress in Black (LBD):

A staple of any woman's closet, the Little Black Dress is both classic and timeless. It's the height of sophistication, with countless style options for formal gatherings and cocktail parties alike.

3. Customised Trousers:

A sophisticated wardrobe staple is a well-tailored pair of neutral-colored trousers. These trousers serve as a base for a variety of sophisticated and adaptable ensembles, whether they are worn for business or stylish informal occasions.

4. The Everlasting Trench Coat:

A timeless trench coat elevates any ensemble and is appropriate for every season. Its classic style makes it suitable for both formal and casual outfits, making it a must-have piece of outerwear.

5. Coat of leather:

Your outfit gains an edge with a leather jacket, which exudes style and rebelliousness. It easily updates your appearance whether it's draped over a dress or worn with jeans.

6. Silk Turtleneck:

A silk blouse is a representation of refined understatement. It is appropriate for both formal settings and special occasions thanks to its opulent texture and classic appeal.

7. Accessories with Pearls:

Pearls are always in style. A pearl necklace or pair of pearl earrings may give refinement to any ensemble and are a reliable and traditional choice for an accessory.

8. Customised Blazer:

Any outfit looks more polished when the blazer is well-fitting. It can be dressed up or down. For a business casual style, wear it with trousers or jeans.

9. The Ideal Jeans Pair:

For their comfort and adaptability, a well-fitting pair of jeans is a wardrobe staple. Jeans are a classic and useful option, whether they're dressed up with heels or down with trainers.

10. Soft Ballet Slippers:

Ballet flats are an essential footwear choice because they are stylish and cozy. They are a versatile and fashionable option for daily wear that goes well with a wide range of ensembles.

"Timeless Wardrobe Essentials for Every Woman" is an encouragement to invest in pieces that complement one's style, endure the ebb and flow of trends, and capture the timeless elegance that characterizes timeless fashion, rather than just a fashion guide.

CHAPTER 6: EMBRACING CHANGE: REDEFINING BEAUTY STANDARDS

Embracing Change: Redefining Beauty Standards" captures Vanessa Williams's liberating philosophy, which questions accepted ideas and exhorts people to accept their changing selves with grace and confidence. This idea boldly declares that beauty is ageless and that every stage of life offers a chance for self-realization and reinvention.

Vanessa's interpretation of "Embracing Change" appreciates the transforming potential that comes with it rather than opposing the way time moves naturally. This idea encourages people to reevaluate beauty standards by realizing that genuine appeal stems from perseverance, genuineness, and a readiness to accept life's unavoidable changes.

"Embracing Change" emerges as a groundbreaking idea in a culture that is frequently preoccupied with youthful appearances. Vanessa Williams is an advocate for a different kind of viewpoint, one that views life's obstacles as chances for personal development, grey hair as a crown of knowledge, and wrinkles as lines of experience. It's a call to reject conventional norms and embrace the beauty that arises from navigating life's always-shifting terrain.

By encouraging people to see change as a catalyst for self-discovery, this principle enables people to embrace their newly discovered strengths and recognize the beauty that comes with resilience. Inspiring people to rewrite their stories about beauty, reinterpret social norms, and develop ageless confidence, Vanessa's vision is a call to action.

"Embracing Change" is essentially a celebration of the beauty that arises from accepting and embracing life's unavoidable changes. This ideology exhorts people to take pride in their paths, stand tall, and acknowledge that every transition presents a chance to redefine what it means to be genuinely beautiful. Vanessa Williams uses this idea to encourage people to go on a path of self-acceptance, love, and the deep beauty that appears when we accept the always-shifting fabric of our lives.

6:1 Vanessa Williams's Advocacy for Age-Inclusive Beauty

"Vanessa Williams's Advocacy for Age-Inclusive Beauty" is a compelling example of her dedication to changing how society views aging and beauty. This activism challenges the conventional narrative that frequently marginalizes people as they age and serves as a light for inclusivity.

Vanessa is an advocate for age-inclusive beauty who goes above and beyond the surface in her quest to dismantle age-related preconceptions and redefine societal norms. This advocacy calls for representation that is diverse and encourages sectors to highlight and promote the beauty that cuts beyond generational lines.

The fundamental tenet of this concept is that beauty is a timeless attribute that blossoms with age, experience, confidence, and wisdom. It is not limited to youth. Vanessa Williams is an advocate for a society in which people of all ages are recognized for their inherent beauty and appreciated for it. Her vision encourages people going through different stages of life to feel empowered and worthy.

Vanessa advocates for a paradigm shift in the beauty and fashion industry by pushing for models and ambassadors who represent a wide range of ages. Vanessa Williams is a trailblazer in advancing a culture that honors and honors people at every stage of their lives by dispelling ageist stereotypes and encouraging a more inclusive definition of beauty.

Vanessa Williams's Advocacy for Age-Inclusive Beauty is essentially a visionary endeavor to build a more tolerant and inclusive society—one that acknowledges the strength of experiences, the beauty in wrinkles, and the attraction that comes with age. It's a strong movement that promotes a sense of self-love and confidence that goes beyond social standards by encouraging people to accept their age with pride.

6.2 Breaking Barriers: The Power of Ageless Confidence

Vanessa Williams espouses a revolutionary concept called "Breaking Barriers: The Power of Ageless Confidence," which embodies the strength that results from accepting one's age with unflinching self-assurance. This idea celebrates the strength and grace inherent in self-assurance that surpasses social norms and dispels age-related misconceptions.

Vanessa's support of "Breaking Barriers" goes beyond outward manifestations, stressing the resilience that accompanies timeless confidence on the inside. It's an exhortation to challenge social conventions, smash stereotypes, and bravely move through a society that occasionally imposes age-based restrictions.

People are encouraged by this ideology to acknowledge their inherent power at every stage of life. It's proof that confidence doesn't just come from young people; it's a trait that develops with age and becomes an enduring source of strength when faced with obstacles. Vanessa Williams encourages an attitude that sees growing older as a strength, a wellspring of knowledge, and a springboard for self-assurance.

"Breaking Barriers" is a call to change the story and maintain the conviction that confidence grows with time. It's a statement that power and beauty are determined by unwavering self-assurance derived from a life well-lived, not by a numerical value. Vanessa's mission calls on people to value their uniqueness, defy social norms, and embody the uplifting spirit of timeless confidence.

"Breaking Barriers: The Power of Ageless Confidence" is essentially a call to action for people to take ownership of their power and resist social pressure to do so. It promotes a way of thinking that engenders resilience, self-love, and unwavering confidence that knows no age limits, opening doors to the boundless possibilities that come with facing each chapter of life with bravery and grace.

CHAPTER 7: BEAUTY BEYOND BORDERS

Vanessa Williams espouses the enthralling concept of "Beauty Beyond Borders," which transcends cultural barriers and honors the varied fabric of beauty present throughout the world. This principle acknowledges that all cultures add to the rich tapestry of global attraction and that beauty is a universal language that transcends national boundaries.

Vanessa's concept of "Beauty Beyond Borders" fosters an awareness that extends beyond outward looks by encouraging people to discover and value beauty practices from all civilizations. It's a call to accept the distinctiveness of many customs, practices, and viewpoints on what constitutes beauty.

This way of thinking celebrates diversity by realizing that there are many different ways to exhibit beauty and that it is not limited to one ideal. "Beauty Beyond Borders" encourages people to absorb, be motivated by, and incorporate ageless beauty rituals and secrets from many cultures.

Beyond aesthetics, Vanessa Williams's support of "Beauty Beyond Borders" is a call to harmony, respect for one another, and a common understanding of the beauty that binds us all. This idealism becomes a potent tool for creating understanding and connections in our global community by dismantling barriers between cultures and encouraging cross-cultural communication.

"Beauty Beyond Borders" is essentially a celebration of the tremendous beauty inherent in human diversity. It invites people to see beyond their cultural viewpoints, value the various ways that beauty is expressed around the world, and embrace a shared vision in which the diversity of our experiences enriches and strengthens the global community.

7:1 Vanessa's Global Beauty Influences

The engrossing "Vanessa's Global Beauty Influences" delves into the many and varied sources that have influenced Vanessa Williams's ageless beauty philosophy. This concept incorporates a rich tapestry of inspirations that cut across cultural boundaries, reflecting her admiration for beauty practices from around the globe.

Vanessa's admiration for beauty around the world is evidence of her willingness to absorb new information and find inspiration in different cultures. She incorporates the greatest beauty advice from other cultures into her routine, incorporating it into everything from skincare routines to makeup methods and beyond. This theory combines the most beloved and successful beauty secrets into a comprehensive strategy that is time-tested.

This idea celebrates each beauty practice's cultural relevance, history, and customs rather than focusing only on cosmetics and methods. Vanessa's impacts on global beauty highlight the beauty that results from accepting diversity and appreciating the distinctive contributions made by other civilizations to the realm of glitz.

Vanessa Williams inspires people to explore new ideas, widen their horizons, and value the diversity that results from a worldwide interchange of beauty customs by fusing global beauty inspirations into her philosophy. It's a voyage of inspiration that promotes an understanding of the transformational power of beauty practices from all over the world beyond cultural boundaries.

"Vanessa's Global Beauty Influences" is essentially a celebration of the international language of beauty, serving as a reminder that true beauty transcends national boundaries. Encouraging people to discover, educate themselves about, and draw inspiration from the various and ageless beauty practices that enhance our

common human experience, fosters a collective
appreciation for the world's rich tapestry of beauty.

7:2 Timeless Beauty Practices from Around the World

The fascinating study "Timeless Beauty Practises from Around the World" delves into the many timeless beauty routines that have survived across centuries and cultural divides. This school of thought acknowledges that great beauty transcends all boundaries and honors the knowledge that has been passed down through the ages.

This ideology bears witness to the diverse range of global beauty practices, encompassing the holistic skincare traditions of Japan, the Ayurvedic principles of India, and the natural beauty secrets of indigenous populations. It represents the idea that classic beauty is a universal idea and that every culture has a special way of nourishing and developing an individual's inherent beauty.

The tenets of "Timeless Beauty Practises from Around the World" go beyond appearances, frequently embracing holistic methods that highlight the relationship between the body, mind, and spirit. Beauty is a multifaceted and holistic concept, which is reinforced by various beauty traditions, which may involve the use of natural products, thoughtful rituals, or age-old wellness practices.

People can access a wealth of knowledge that goes far beyond current fashions by investigating and adopting these age-old beauty practices. It's an invitation to absorb knowledge from the various civilizations that have developed their distinct standards of beauty, fostering an international knowledge exchange that broadens our perspective of what it is to be exquisitely timeless.

"Timeless Beauty Practises from Around the World" is essentially a tribute to the timeless appeal of the many cultural beauty customs. It encourages people to view beauty more holistically and globally, realizing that the foundations of enduring beauty are built into the very fabric of many cultures.

CHAPTER 8: AGE-DEFYING WISDOM FROM VANESSA'S INNER CIRCLE

"Age-Defying Wisdom from Vanessa's Inner Circle" is a singular and personal examination of the thoughts and experiences that Vanessa Williams' closest friends and family have shared. Beyond personal beauty regimens, this philosophy explores the common knowledge, routines, and viewpoints that give her trusted inner circle its timeless appeal.

Vanessa's inner circle consists of a wide range of people, including mentors, confidantes, friends, and beauty gurus, all of whom have influenced her classic approach to aging. The collective knowledge of this inner circle turns into a wealth of age-defying techniques that provide a comprehensive understanding of what it takes to keep elegance and beauty across time.

This ideology focuses on the mindset, way of life, and support networks that enhance people's general well-being in addition to outward beauty regimens. It emphasizes how crucial it is to surround oneself with positive people, cultivate relationships, and be a part of an inspiring and uplifted group.

"Age-Defying Wisdom from Vanessa's Inner Circle" gives readers an insight into the experiences of people who have followed Vanessa's path and, consequently, been impacted by her ageless beauty mantra. It's an admission that age-defying beauty is frequently a team effort enhanced by the combined knowledge of a close-knit support system rather than a solitary one.

This ideology is essentially a celebration of the connections between healing, beauty, and the strength that arises from shared experiences. It inspires people to build their strong inner networks, realizing the transformational potential of collective knowledge in the quest for timeless beauty and unwavering self-assurance.

8:1 Interviews with Beauty Experts and Collaborators

"Interviews with Beauty Experts and Collaborators" provides an insight into the realm of knowledge and teamwork that has influenced Vanessa Williams's enduring journey through beauty. Vanessa's approach to timeless beauty has been greatly influenced and refined by the aggregate expertise and ideas of industry professionals, beauty experts, and partners, all of whom are represented in this philosophy.

Readers can discover a plethora of unconventional beauty practices, insider knowledge, and beauty wisdom through these interviews. Vanessa's willingness to work together with subject matter specialists results in lively discussions where the most recent innovations, trends, and tried-and-true methods are shared.

This way of thinking supports the notion that beauty is a dynamic environment enhanced by the knowledge and imagination of those who commit their life to the search for artistic greatness. These interviews with skin care specialists, makeup artists, hairstylists, and wellness experts offer a thorough overview of the diverse realm of beauty.

"Interviews with Beauty Experts and Collaborators" emphasizes the value of cooperation and ongoing education in the field of beauty in addition to being an instructional tool. It's a motivational voyage that inspires readers to look for different viewpoints, keep up with business advancements, and accept the collective wisdom that results from teamwork.

This idea is, at its core, an homage to the spirit of cooperation that characterizes the beauty industry. It encourages a greater comprehension of the always-changing realm of timeless beauty by allowing people to explore, learn from, and be inspired by the perspectives of those at the forefront of beauty innovation.

8:2 Personal Stories of Transformation and Empowerment

The heartfelt investigation of the enormous influence Vanessa Williams's timeless beauty philosophy has had on people's lives may be found in "Personal Stories of Transformation and Empowerment". This way of thinking transcends beauty standards and dives into stories of empowerment, resiliency, and personal development.

Readers can see a glimpse into the life-changing experiences of those who have adopted Vanessa's ideals through these personal anecdotes. These stories illustrate the various ways that timeless beauty is a reflection of inner strength, self-assurance, and a deep sense of self rather than just a physical quality.

"Personal Stories of Transformation and Empowerment" emphasizes the beauty that results from conquering obstacles, accepting change, and gracefully negotiating life's curveballs. It becomes a collective testament to the notion that beauty is an expression of the bravery and resiliency that may be found within rather than being limited to outward appearances.

This idea encourages people to perceive their own transformational stories as essential to their attractiveness by providing them with a powerful story. It's an ode to originality, recognizing that each setback, victory, and developmental milestone adds to the distinct charm that ages with time.

"Personal Stories of Transformation and Empowerment" is essentially a reminder that genuine beauty is an extremely intimate and life-changing experience. People get inspiration, a sense of community, and a sense of empowerment from these stories because they see how their own stories fit into the larger, timeless beauty.

CONCLUSION

As we come to the end of the engrossing investigation found in "Vanessa Williams's Queen of Timeless Beauty: Age-Defying Wisdom and Beauty Secrets," we find ourselves on the cusp of a journey that has the power to transform. This journey surpasses traditional ideas of beauty, challenges social norms, and honors the timeless beauty that every person possesses.

In this book, we've explored the principles of everlasting beauty, accepted the importance of inner brightness, and gleaned ageless knowledge from Vanessa's routine and international sources. We've talked about mindful aging and its profound beauty, fitness routines, makeup magic, and skincare habits. Together, we've dismantled barriers, embraced age-inclusive beauty, and honored style and elegance throughout history. We've explored the globe, learning about ageless beauty techniques and hearing about individual experiences of empowerment and metamorphosis.

Essentially, this book is an invitation to find and redefine your personal story of beauty rather than just a guide. Beyond just a collection of exercises, Vanessa Williams's Queen of Timeless Beauty concept celebrates your journey, affirms your intrinsic value, and exhorts you to face each stage of life with poise and confidence.

As you close these pages, keep in mind that your timeless appeal is a reflection of your uniqueness, fortitude, and perseverance rather than an unattainable ideal. Allow the knowledge imparted in these chapters to motivate you to develop inner brightness, showcase your distinct style, and face aging with courage.

It's a celebration of your everlasting beauty that you are pursuing immortal brilliance. I hope this book serves as a roadmap, a friend, and a source of motivation for you as you set out on this empowering journey. The Queen of Timeless Beauty philosophy will be your constant companion as you embark on your journey of age-defying elegance. It will point you in the direction of a life full of self-assurance, genuineness, and endless appeal.

We are grateful that you let Vanessa Williams's ageless beauty secrets play a role in your life-changing experience. May you embrace your reign as the Queen of Timeless Beauty and may the light that emanates from within you shine brightly along your way.